COTSWOLDS TRAVEL GUIDE 2025

Discover England's Charming Countryside and Immersive Cultural Experiences with Detailed Maps, Cycling, and Walking Routes.

By

Aspen B. Alderwood

Copyright 2025 Aspen B. Alderwood All Rights Reserved

Any reproduction of this work, in part or whole, is strictly forbidden without express written permission from the publisher or author, regardless of the format (written, electronic, audio, or visual). Limited exceptions exist for brief quotations in reviews or articles, and for cases with specific authorization. While every effort has been made to ensure accuracy, the author and publisher disclaim responsibility for potential errors or omissions and any resulting consequences.

Disclaimer: The costs mentioned in this guide were current at the time of publication. However, prices for services, lodging, and attractions may fluctuate. We suggest allocating additional funds to cover potential increases. Many factors beyond our control can affect travel costs, so we recommend verifying current prices and adjusting your budget as needed for a stress-free journey. We hope you have a safe and enjoyable trip!

Cotswolds in Pixels (1)

Cotswolds in Pixels (2)

Cotswolds in Pixels (3)

5 | Cotswolds Travel Guide 2025

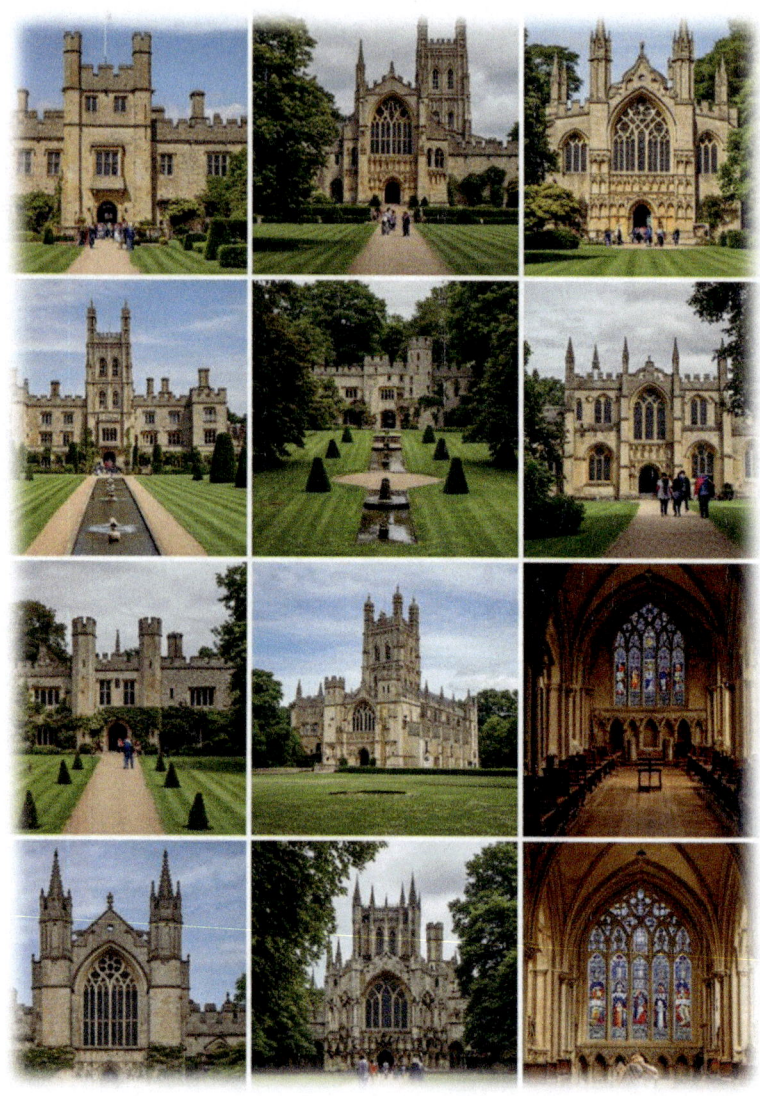

Cotswolds in Pixels (4)

TABLE OF CONTENT

INTRODUCTION — 13

WELCOME TO A TIMELESS ESCAPE INTO ENGLAND'S IDYLLIC COUNTRYSIDE — 13
WHY VISIT IN 2025? NEW EXPERIENCES, TIMELESS CHARM, AND SUSTAINABLE INNOVATIONS. — 14
THE COTSWOLDS AONB: A UNESCO-PROTECTED LANDSCAPE OF ROLLING HILLS AND HERITAGE. — 15
HISTORY AND ARCHITECTURE: FROM ROMAN ROOTS TO HONEY-HUED STONE COTTAGES. — 16
SUSTAINABLE TRAVEL IN 2025: PRESERVING BEAUTY THROUGH ECO-CONSCIOUS TOURISM. — 17
A PERSONAL INVITATION. — 18

CHAPTER ONE — 19

PLANNING YOUR COTSWOLDS ADVENTURE — 19
WHEN TO VISIT: SEASONAL FESTIVALS, WILDFLOWER BLOOMS, AND WINTER MAGIC. — 19
WEATHER INSIGHTS & PACKING TIPS: GEAR FOR COUNTRYSIDE EXPLORATION. — 21
BUDGETING FOR 2025: FROM LUXURY RETREATS TO COZY FARM STAYS. — 22
POST-BREXIT TRAVEL REQUIREMENTS: VISAS, PASSPORTS, AND HEALTH INSURANCE. — 23
LOCAL ETIQUETTE: RESPECTING VILLAGE LIFE AND COUNTRYSIDE TRADITIONS. — 23

Travel Insurance: Coverage for Hiking, Cycling, and Historic Stays. 24
A Parting Word from Your (Slightly Muddy) Guide. 25

CHAPTER TWO 27

Getting to and around the Cotswolds 27
Arriving in 2025: Airports, Rails, and the Green Revolution. 27
Car Rentals: Mastering the Art of the Hedge Hug. 30
Cycling: Pedal-Powered Poetry 31
Walking: Where Boots Meet Soul 32
Seasonal Tips: Navigating Nature's Moods. 32
A Final Word from Your Road-Weary (But Heart-Full) Guide. 33

CHAPTER THREE 35

Themed Itineraries 35
Romantic 4-Day Escape: Hot Air Balloon Rides and Private Castle Dinners. 36
Family 5-Day Fun: Cotswold Wildlife Park and Model Village Explorations. 37
7-Day Cultural Deep Dive: Shakespearean Plays and Georgian Architecture. 39
Photography Tour: Golden Hour at Broadway Tower, Lavender Fields at Snowshill. 42
A Parting Snap 43

CHAPTER FOUR 45

ACCOMMODATION GUIDE	**45**
LODGING STYLES	45
BOUTIQUE HOTELS: 2025'S FRESH FACES	47
QUAINT B&BS AND DOG-FRIENDLY COTTAGES.	48
ECO-GLAMPING AND SOLAR-POWERED FARM STAY.	50
CHIPPING CAMPDEN: GATEWAY TO THE COTSWOLD WAY.	51
CHELTENHAM: REGENCY ELEGANCE AND FESTIVAL HUB.	52
TETBURY: ROYAL CONNECTIONS AND ANTIQUE TREASURES.	53
A FINAL TIP FROM YOUR COTSWOLDS CONFIDANT	54

CHAPTER FIVE   55

ICONIC COTSWOLDS EXPERIENCES	**55**
MUST-SEE VILLAGES: TIMELESS BEAUTY IN EVERY COBBLESTONE.	56
HISTORIC ESTATES: PALACES, CASTLES, AND ROYAL GARDENS	58
GARDENS & NATURE: BLOOMS, ARBORETUMS, AND WILD WONDERS.	61
ARCHITECTURAL GEMS: FROM SAXON SIMPLICITY TO WOOL CHURCH GRANDEUR.	63
2025 HIGHLIGHTS: NEW REASONS TO FALL IN LOVE.	64
A FINAL WORD FROM YOUR COTSWOLDS COMPANION.	66

CHAPTER SIX   67

CULTURAL EXPERIENCES	**67**
MUSEUMS: TIME TRAVEL THROUGH ARTIFACTS AND CRAFT.	67
FESTIVALS: CELEBRATE LIKE A LOCAL.	69
PERFORMING ARTS: CURTAIN UP IN THE COUNTRYSIDE.	71
A CULTURAL CURTAIN CALL	73

CHAPTER SEVEN   75

CULINARY ADVENTURES	**75**
FARM-TO-TABLE: SOIL TO SOUL DINING	75
LOCAL FLAVORS: TASTE CENTURIES OF TRADITION	77
PUBS & DINING: FROM ANCIENT ALEHOUSES TO MICHELIN STARS.	79
TOURS: SIP, SWIRL, AND SAVOR.	81
A FINAL TOAST FROM YOUR CULINARY GUIDE	82

CHAPTER EIGHT   83

SHOPPING AND LOCAL CRAFTS	**83**
ANTIQUE HAVENS: TREASURES WITH TALES	83
ARTISAN MARKETS: WHERE LOCALS STOCK THEIR LARDERS.	85
WOOL HERITAGE: FROM FLEECE TO FASHION.	86
A FINAL WORD FROM YOUR SHOPPING SHERPA	88

CHAPTER NINE   89

PRACTICAL INFORMATION	**89**
EMERGENCIES: STAYING SAFE IN THE SLOW LANE	89
ACCESSIBILITY: EXPLORING WITHOUT LIMITS	91
SAFETY: COTSWOLDS COMMONSENSE.	92
LOCAL LINGO: COTSWOLDS DICTIONARY	92
TRANSPORT TIMETABLES: 2025 UPDATES.	93
A PARTING WORD FROM YOUR COTSWOLDS CONFIDANT.	94

CONCLUSION   95

WHERE TIME LINGERS AND FOOTPRINTS FADE	**95**
PARTING THOUGHTS: EMBRACING SLOW TRAVEL IN A FAST-PACED WORLD.	95

YOUR ROLE IN PRESERVATION: LEAVING LIGHT FOOTPRINTS FOR
FUTURE GENERATIONS.   96
A FINAL TOAST TO YOUR COTSWOLDS JOURNEY   97

INTRODUCTION

Welcome to a Timeless Escape into England's Idyllic Countryside

Y ou're standing on a sunlit lane in Bibury, a village so achingly perfect it feels plucked from a watercolor painting. The morning mist clings to the River Coln like lace, and the only sounds are the soft clop of a horse-drawn cart and the distant bleat of sheep grazing on emerald hills. The air smells of freshly cut grass and woodsmoke, mingling with the warm, buttery scent of scones drifting from a cottage window. This is the Cotswold —a place where time slows, where every stone, meadow, and hedgerow whispers stories of centuries past.

I first stumbled into this magical corner of England on a misty autumn morning years ago, my boots crunching golden leaves as I wandered the streets of Bourton-on-the-Water. The village's low-arched bridges and honey-hued cottages glowed like amber in the dawn light, and I felt an instant, almost primal connection to the landscape. It wasn't just the beauty that gripped me; it was the *feeling* of the Cotswold—a soul-deep serenity, as if the hills themselves were exhaling peace into the world.

This isn't just a destination. It's an invitation to step into a living postcard, where every winding lane leads to discovery. Whether you're sipping cider in a 15th-century pub, tracing Roman mosaics in Cirencester, or simply sitting under an ancient yew tree in Stow-on-the-Wold's churchyard, the Cotswolds wraps you in a sense of belonging. And in 2025, this timeless escape feels more vital than ever.

Why Visit in 2025? New Experiences, Timeless Charm, and Sustainable Innovations.

"Why now?" you might ask. Because 2025 is the year the Cotswolds harmonizes its rich past with an exciting, eco-conscious future. Imagine wandering through Blenheim Palace's newly restored Baroque gardens, then cycling to a zero-waste pop-up café in a converted barn, where your coffee grounds will fertilize lavender fields. Or attending the inaugural "Cotswolds Green Festival" in Cheltenham, where local cheesemakers, solar-powered breweries, and hedge-laying artisans showcase innovations rooted in tradition.

But fear not—the soul of the Cotswolds remains untouched. The same villages that charmed **J.R.R.** Tolkien and Jane Austen still beckon with cobblestone charm. In 2025, you'll find fresh reasons to fall in love: a reopened Roman villa in Chedworth with augmented reality tours, or a new stretch of the Cotswold Way linking forgotten hamlets. Yet, what truly sets this year apart is how communities are pioneering sustainability without sacrificing character. Farmers are reviving ancient crop rotations, inns are harnessing geothermal energy, and even the iconic woolen mills now spin yarn from carbon-neutral flocks.

This is a moment to witness a landscape evolving thoughtfully, where "progress" means deepening—not diluting—the Cotswolds' magic.

The Cotswolds AONB: A UNESCO-Protected Landscape of Rolling Hills and Heritage.

Let me take you back to a crisp spring morning when I hiked the Cotswold Way near Broadway Tower. As I climbed, the world unfolded beneath me: patchwork fields stitched with drystone walls, valleys dotted with sheep like cotton balls, and villages clinging to hillsides like swallows' nests. This is the Cotswolds Area of Outstanding Natural Beauty (AONB), a UNESCO-recognized tapestry of 790 square miles where every view feels composed by a master artist.

The AONB designation isn't just a badge—it's a covenant between land and people. Farmers here still practice "ridge and furrow" medieval ploughing to protect soil; volunteers' clear paths through bluebell woods so hikers tread lightly; and villages like Painswick limit streetlights to preserve starry skies. In 2025, new "Wildlife Corridors" will link fragmented habitats, allowing otters to reclaim trout-filled streams and red kites to soar over regenerated hedgerows.

But the true genius of this landscape is how it invites you to become part of its rhythm. Join a dawn "bird census" in the Slad Valley, where Laurie Lee's **Cider With Rosie** still echoes in the meadows. Or follow the "Wildflower Way," a 2025-launched trail where orchids and cowslips paint the banks of the Windrush River. The Cotswolds doesn't just want your admiration—it asks for your partnership in its preservation.

History and Architecture: From Roman Roots to Honey-Hued Stone Cottages.

Beneath the bucolic surface lies a land steeped in drama. Two thousand years ago, the Cotswolds were the Roman Empire's woolen heartland. Stand in Cirencester's Corinium Museum, and you'll face a mosaic of Medusa, her stone eyes glaring from a villa floor—a reminder that this quiet market town was once Britannia's second-largest city. Later, medieval wool merchants funneled fortunes into "wool churches" like Northleach's St. Peter and St. Paul, where gargoyles snarl above tombs of sheep-magnates.

But it's the cottages that steal hearts. That golden hue? It's Jurassic limestone, quarried locally and weathering to a honey-gold that glows in afternoon light. I'll never forget bunking in a 17th-century weaver's cottage in Chipping Campden, its walls two feet thick, its fireplace big enough to roast a boar. As rain pattered outside, I traced initials carved by long-dead residents into beams—a visceral link to lives woven into these stones.

In 2025, history isn't just preserved; it's alive. Participate in a Roman cookery workshop at Chedworth Villa, or help rebuild a drystone wall using techniques unchanged since the Iron Age. New interactive trails, like "Tolkien's Cotswolds," reveal how the Shire's rolling hills were born right here in villages like Moreton-in-Marsh.

Sustainable Travel in 2025: Preserving Beauty Through Eco-Conscious Tourism.

Here's the secret the Cotswolds guards jealously: its beauty is fragile. Those picture-perfect villages can't withstand hordes of gas-guzzling coaches. That's why 2025 marks a bold leap in sustainable travel—one that lets you indulge without guilt.

Stay in a Grade II-listed barn near Stroud, now a carbon-neutral retreat heated by geothermal springs. Dine at pubs like The Bell Inn in Langford, where menus feature "forgotten" vegetables grown in no-till gardens. Even your souvenirs can be green: commission a bespoke willow basket from the last master craftsman in the Coln Valley, or adopt a heritage-breed sheep whose wool funds rewilding projects.

Transport? Ditch the car. New electric bike hubs in Bourton-on-the-Water offer GPS-guided routes to organic vineyards and train stations with hourly "green carriages" to London. And if you're craving luxury, the 2025-opened "Eden Cottage" in Blockley proves sustainability isn't Spartan—think rainwater infinity pools and Michelin-starred vegan feasts.

A Personal Invitation.

The Cotswolds is more than a place—it's a state of mind. It's the thrill of cresting a hill to find a village unchanged in 300 years. It's the warmth of a farmer waving you through a gate as his sheep scatter like spilled pearls. It's the quiet pride of a potter in Winchcombe, her hands shaping clay as her ancestors did when Henry VIII ruled.

In 2025, we're not just visitors here. We're stewards. So come, tread softly, linger long, and let these ancient hills work their gentle alchemy on your soul. The kettle's always on, the footpaths are beckoning, and the Cotswolds is ready to welcome you home.

CHAPTER ONE

Planning Your Cotswolds Adventure

Let me confess something: I'm a hopeless over-packer. On my first Cotswolds trip, I arrived with a suitcase so overstuffed it could've housed a family of hedgehogs. But here's what I've learned: the magic of this place isn't in what you bring—it's in how you prepare. Think of this chapter as your trusty map, your well-worn walking stick, and your local pub confidant all rolled into one. Let's craft an adventure that's as seamless as the curve of a drystone wall.

When to Visit: Seasonal Festivals, Wildflower Blooms, and Winter Magic.

The Cotswolds doesn't just change with the seasons—it revels in them. I've danced through bluebell woods in spring, sipped cider in sunflower fields in summer, crunch-tested every autumn leaf between Stow and Slad, and huddled by roaring fires in snow-dusted inns. Here's why 2025 is your year:

Spring (March–May):

Picture this: You're knee-deep in a sea of bluebills at the Wychwood Forest near Shipton-under-Wychwood, their violet haze stretching like a bruise across the woodland floor. April brings the Cheltenham Poetry Festival, where bards recite verses in honey-stone courtyards. Don't miss the Tetbury Woolsack Races (May 5th), where locals haul 60-pound wool sacks up Gumstool Hill—a tradition born from medieval wool taxes. Pro tip: Visit the Westonbirt Arboretum in late April when magnolias erupt like pink fireworks.

Summer (June–August):

The Cotswolds becomes a living postcard. June's Broadway Arts Festival transforms this golden village into an open-air gallery. July? Head to Cotswold Farm Park (Adam Henson's ode to rare breeds) for lambing demos and hay-bale picnics. But my heart belongs to August's Painswick Feast Week, where locals parade a 10-foot **"Pig of Painswick"** (a bread-and-apple monstrosity) through streets lined with fairy lights.

Autumn (September–November):

This is when the landscape blushes. Join the Stroud Valleys Artisans Trail (Sept 13–15), where potters, weavers, and blacksmiths fling open their studio doors. October's Sudeley Castle Apple Festival lets you press cider beside Henry VIII's former hunting grounds. For spine-tingling charm, visit Lower Slaughter in late November—its mill pond mirrors scarlet and gold trees like a liquid tapestry.

Winter (December–February):

Yes, it's cold. Yes, it's magical. Christmas at Blenheim Palace (through Dec 30th) turns Capability Brown's gardens into a luminescent wonderland. On Twelfth Night (Jan 5th), join villagers in Chipping Campden to wassail orchards with cider-soaked toast (to appease apple tree spirits, naturally). And February? Cozy up at The Porch House in Stow-on-the-Wold—England's oldest inn—with a mulled wine that's been perfected since 947 AD.

Weather Insights & Packing Tips: Gear for Countryside Exploration.

The Cotswolds' weather is as whimsical as a Morris dancer's handkerchief. Last May, I sunbathed in Broadway one afternoon and dodged hailstones in Bourton the next. Here's your survival kit:

- **Clothing:** Layers, layers, layers: A merino wool base, fleece mid-layer, and waterproof shell are non-negotiable.
- **Footwear:** Blundstone boots (ankle support for stiles) + foldable Wellies (for boggy fields).
- **Accessories:** A waxed-cotton hat (dodges rain and sheep stares) and fingerless gloves (for camera-ready hands).
- **Portable phone charger:** Villages like Snowshill still charm with spotty reception.
- **Ordnance Survey Map OL45:** Because nothing beats tracing your finger along the Cotswold Way when your GPS fails.
- **Reusable water bottle:** Refill at village taps marked "Drinking Water for Walkers."

<u>**Pro Tip:**</u> Pack a small umbrella not for rain, but for navigating narrow shop aisles in Burford without knocking over £50 ceramic badgers.

Budgeting for 2025: From Luxury Retreats to Cozy Farm Stays.

The Cotswolds caters to both hedonists and penny-pinchers. Let's break it down:

Luxury (£300+/night):

- **Barnsley House (Cirencester):** Soak in the 2025-renovated Secret Garden Spa after a private tour of their zero-waste kitchen.
- **Thyme Manor (Southrop):** Their new "Shepherd's Bothy" suite includes a flock of sheep you can "borrow" for meadow picnics.

Mid-Range (£120–£250/night):

- **The Fish Hotel (Broadway):** Treehouse suites with bathtubs overlooking Broadway Tower.
- **Eco-Pod Glamping (Near Northleach):** Solar-heated geodesic domes with vintage record players.

Budget (Under £100/night):

- **Wold Farm Stay (Near Moreton-in-Marsh):** Milk cows at dawn, then feast on farmhouse fry-ups. £60/night, cash only.
- **YHA Stow-on-the-Wold:** Bunk in a 16th-century townhouse. Pro tip: Book the "Priest's Hole" room—a smuggler's hideaway.

Dining:

- **Splurge:** Lumière (Cheltenham)—7-course tasting menus with foraged nettle risotto (£95pp).

> **Save:** Huffkins Bakery chain—£5 for a Gloucester Old Spot sausage roll and a "slice of heaven" (their words) lemon drizzle cake.

Post-Brexit Travel Requirements: Visas, Passports, and Health Insurance.

As of 2025, the rules are clearer than a Cotswold spring:

> **Passports:** Must be valid for at least 6 months beyond your stay. No stamps needed for stays under 90 days (for most non-EU nationals).
> **Visas:** USA/Canada/Australia. No visa required for stays up to 6 months.
> **EU Citizens:** Visa-free for 90 days, but you'll need an ETIAS authorization (apply online pre-trip).
> **Health Insurance:** The NHS won't cover you. Get a policy that includes hiking accidents (I once slipped on a stile and needed a £200 X-ray in Cirencester Hospital).

Pro Tip: Carry a GHIC card (EU citizens) for reduced emergency care costs.

Local Etiquette: Respecting Village Life and Countryside Traditions.

The Cotswolds runs on quiet courtesy. Here's how to blend in:

- ➢ **Greetings:** A nod and "Lovely day, isn't it?" opens doors. Avoid loud phone chats in villages—you'll scandalize the postmistress.
- ➢ **Gates:** If you open it, close it. If it's closed, leave it. Farmers still shoot trespassers (with disapproving glares).
- ➢ **Pubs:** Order at the bar, even in posh gastropubs. Tip 10% only if service was exceptional.
- ➢ **Photography:** Ask before snapping cottages—that's someone's home, not a film set.
- ➢ **Driving:** Reverse into passing spots on single-track lanes. Wave thanks—it's the law (unofficially).

Travel Insurance: Coverage for Hiking, Cycling, and Historic Stays.

Let's get real: You're more likely to sprain an ankle on a stile than get kidnapped by a sheep. Ensure your policy covers:

- ➢ **Emergency evacuation:** Some trails (e.g., Cleeve Hill) require airlift access.
- ➢ **Historic accommodation quirks:** I once tripped over a wonky floorboard in a Chipping Campden B&B— the insurance paid for my new camera lens.
- ➢ **E-bike rentals:** The Cotswold Way's hills are no joke.
- ➢ **Cancellations:** Festivals like the **Cheltenham Literature Festival** sell out fast—insure those tickets.

<u>Pro Tip:</u> Use **Battleface** or **World Nomads**—they specialize in adventure coverage.

A Parting Word from Your (Slightly Muddy) Guide.

Planning a Cotswolds trip is like baking a proper Victoria sponge: It requires patience, good ingredients, and a willingness to embrace glorious messiness. I still remember my first ill-planned jaunt—I wore city shoes, got lost in a rainstorm, and ended up sharing a ploughman's lunch with a retired sheepdog breeder in a pub near Naunton. It was perfect.

So, pack your sense of wonder, leave room for serendipity, and trust that these hills have been welcoming wayward souls for centuries. Your adventure starts now—and I'll be right here, map in hand, ready to whisper, **"You see that footpath? Let's follow it."**

CHAPTER TWO

Getting to and around the Cotswolds

Let me tell you about the time I arrived in the Cotswolds with a suitcase full of city impatience. Fresh off a delayed flight, I rented a car, white-knuckled my way down a lane narrower than a shepherd's footpath, and promptly got stuck behind a flock of sheep migrating to greener pastures. But here's the secret I learned that day: **"getting there is half the magic"**. The Cotswolds rewards those who embrace the journey as much as the destination. So, let's chart your course through this pastoral wonderland—whether you arrive by train, tyre, or tiptoe.

Arriving in 2025: Airports, Rails, and the Green Revolution.

Airports: Gateways to the Golden Countryside

The Cotswolds doesn't have its own airport, but that's part of its charm—you'll glide into modernity before slipping into timelessness. Here's your 2025 cheat sheet:

- **Bristol Airport (1 hour drive):** My personal favorite. New in 2025: a dedicated EV shuttle to Cheltenham, charging while you marvel at the Severn Valley. Pro tip: Grab a Proper Cornish pasty at arrivals—it'll tide you over till your first cream tea.

Bristol Airport to Cheltenham by Road

- **Birmingham Airport (1.5 hours):** Ideal for transatlantic travelers. The AirRail Link now whisks you to Birmingham New Street Station in 8 minutes, where direct trains to Moreton-in-Marsh await.
- **London Heathrow (2 hours):** Book the National Express Cotswolds Connector—a plush electric coach with USB-C ports and live commentary on passing landmarks like Blenheim Palace.
- **Manchester Airport (2.5 hours):** Worth it for the Peak District-Cotswolds scenic combo. Rent an EV and take the M6 toll road, stopping at Staffordshire's new Eco-Oasis rest stops (think solar-paneled cafés with lavender lattes).

Train Routes: All Aboard the Time Machine

Nothing beats watching the urban sprawl melt into sheep-dotted hills from a train window. In 2025:

- ➢ **From London Paddington:** Direct GWR (Great Western Railway) services to Kemble (gateway to Cirencester) and Charlbury (for the Evenlode Valley). New this year: Heritage Carriages on select routes—velvet seats, steward service, and stories from conductors who've worked the line since the '80s (the 1880s, they'll joke).
- ➢ **From Birmingham:** The Cotswold Line to Moreton-in-Marsh now offers Cycle Carriages with built-in bike racks. Alight at Honeybourne for a secret footpath to Hidcote Manor's back gates.

From Birmingham New Street to Honeybourne by Rails

Public Buses: The Pulhams Coaches Network

Picture this: You're on the 801 from Cheltenham to Bourton-on-the-Water, rattling past fields where tractors play chicken with pheasants. The driver, Dave (he'll tell you his life story by Stow), pauses to let a heron cross the road. This is rural transit at its finest.

> **Real-Time Apps:** Download Pulhams, "Cotswold Rider" app. It tracks buses via QR codes scanned at stops (yes, even the one shaped like a toadstool in Upper Slaughter).
> **Key Routes:**
- The 855 "Wool & Water" Circuit, which links Northleach's wool church with Bibury's trout farm.
- The 888 "Festival Flyer", summer-only service to Cheltenham's jazz and science fests.

Car Rentals: Mastering the Art of the Hedge Hug.

Driving here is less about speed, more about symbiosis. **Avis** at Gloucester offers Mini Coopers—perfect for lanes where passing requires sucking in your stomach. Avoid SUVs unless you fancy becoming a local legend (see: "The American Who Took Out Mrs. Higgins' Rose Trellis, 2022").

Rules of the Road:

- ✓ **Passing Places:** Reverse into them. It's like chess—anticipate three moves ahead.
- ✓ **Sheep Etiquette:** Stop, smile, snap pics. They're basically woolly traffic lights.

- ✓ **SatNav Warnings:** Ignore shortcuts labeled "Ford." That's a river crossing, not a car brand.

Pro Tip: Rent from Cotswold Classic Cars for a vintage Morris Minor experience. Nothing says "I've arrived" like puttering into Broadway in a 1960s convertible, scarf flapping like a proper Brit.

Cycling: Pedal-Powered Poetry

In 2025, the Cotswold Way's new Circular Routes let you conquer hills without conquering your quads:

- ➢ **E-Bike Rentals:** Cotswold E-Bikes in Winchcombe delivers to your B&B. Their **"Pub & Pedal"** package includes a lock shaped like a horseshoe (to deter tipsy thieves).

Must-Ride Trails:

- ✓ **The Slaughters Circuit (12 miles):** Flat, family-friendly, with a stop at **Lower Slaughter's Old Mill** for blackcurrant sorbet.
- ✓ **Cleeve Hill Climb (Advanced):** Reward your burn with views stretching to Wales and a ploughman's lunch at **The Rising Sun**.

Caution: Dismount for tractors. They're the undisputed kings of these roads.

Walking: Where Boots Meet Soul

This is how the Romans did it—well, minus the Gore-Tex.

- **Trail Maps:** The Cotswolds AONB Authority just launched scratch-and-sniff maps (wild thyme-scented—genius).
- **Guided Rambles:** Join Foot Trails' new **"Wool & Water"** walk. You'll card raw fleece at a 17th-century mill, then toast with damson gin at a lock-keeper's cottage.

Personal Highlight: Last autumn, I followed a badger trail near Stanway House and stumbled upon a hidden Domesday-era chapel. The key? Let curiosity be your compass.

Seasonal Tips: Navigating Nature's Moods.

Winter Wisdom (Dec–Feb):

- ✓ **Road Closures:** Check Gloucestershire County Council's live map. Snowdrifts love blocking the B4077.
- ✓ **Bus Services:** Reduced, but the Cotswold Voluntary Car Scheme pairs you with chatty locals doing school runs.

Summer Strategies (Jun–Aug):

- **Bibury:** Arrive pre-9am or post-6pm. The trout farm's dawn feeding frenzy is better than alarm clocks.
- **Broadway Tower:** Book the Sunset Access slot. You'll have the 360-degree view (and resident peregrines) to yourself.

Insider Hack: Park at Bourton-on-the-Hill and walk 2 miles to Moreton-in-Marsh. You'll bypass the coach conga line.

A Final Word from Your Road-Weary (But Heart-Full) Guide.

I'll never forget the evening I missed the last bus from Stow to Chipping Norton. As I stood pondering my options, a ruddy-cheeked farmer in a Land Rover rolled down his window: "You look like you could use a lift and a pint." An hour later, I was nursing a Hooky Ale in his barn, surrounded by prizewinning sheep and tales of the 2001 foot-and-mouth crisis.

That's the Cotswolds' transport secret: sometimes the best routes aren't on any map. So, pack your patience, charge your sense of wonder, and remember—every wrong turn here leads to a story. Now, let's get you moving. Those hills aren't going to wander themselves.

CHAPTER THREE

Themed Itineraries

Let me let you in on a secret: the Cotswolds isn't just a place—it's a shapeshifter. One moment, it's a stage for lovers whispering under wisteria; the next, a playground for kids chasing ducklings down a stream. Over years of guiding wanderers through these hills, I've learned that the magic lies in *curation*. So, consider this chapter your personal key to unlocking the Cotswolds' many souls. Whether you're here to rekindle romance, ignite curiosity, or chase the perfect light, I've blazed the trails (and maybe tripped over a few stiles) so you don't have to.

Romantic 4-Day Escape: Hot Air Balloon Rides and Private Castle Dinners.

For those who believe love thrives in honey-stone shadows and meadow sunsets.

Day 1: Arrival in Bourton-on-the-Water.

- **Morning:** Check into The Dial House, a 17th-century coaching inn where rooms have freestanding copper tubs and secret garden courtyards.
- **Afternoon:** Stroll the River Windrush hand-in-hand, then share a "Kissing Tart" (raspberry-and-rose custard) at Bakery on the Water.
- **Evening:** Dine at The Rose Tree, where candlelit tables overlook the village's Venetian-style bridges. Order the Cotswold Gold Champagne risotto—it's sprinkled with edible gold leaf, because why not?

Day 2: Soaring Hearts

- **Dawn:** Meet Cotswold Ballooning at 5:30 AM. As you float over Sudeley Castle, pilot Mike (a former RAF navigator) will point out Roman roads snaking through misty fields. Toast with Prosecco mid-air.
- **Afternoon:** Private tour of Bibury's Arlington Row. Bribe the custodian with a £10 "donation" to access the rooftop for a picnic of local Stilton and pear chutney.
- **Evening:** Private Dining at Owlpen Manor. Chef Lydia crafts a 5-course feast in the Tudor kitchen, served under a 400-year-old oak. The **pièce de résistance?** A dessert trolley wheeled in by a butler in period costume.

Day 3: Secrets and Spas

- **Morning:** Couples' massage at Barnsley House's Secret Garden Spa, followed by a dip in their rosemary-infused hydrotherapy pool.
- **Afternoon:** Get lost in Painswick Rococo Garden, where maze-like pathways lead to follies made for stolen kisses.
- **Evening:** Glamping Under the Stars at Luxury Cotswold Camping. Their new 2025 "Sky Domes" have retractable roofs and a hot tub stocked with elderflower gin.

Day 4: Farewell Flourish

- **Morning:** Hire a vintage Morris Minor from Cotswold Classic Cars and drive to Broadway Tower. Climb at sunrise for a 360-degree view of 16 counties.
- **Finale:** Leave a padlock on the "Lovers' Gate" at Snowshill Manor—a 2025 addition where keys are tossed into the lavender fields below.

Family 5-Day Fun: Cotswold Wildlife Park and Model Village Explorations.

For clans who measure joy in ice cream drips and llama cuddles.

Day 1: Arrival in Burford

- **Stay:** The Swan Family Suite, complete with bunk beds shaped like gypsy caravans and a treasure map leading to the hotel's cookie stash.

- **Afternoon:** Feed rainbow trout at Bibury Trout Farm (warning: kids will name them).
- **Evening:** Fish & Chips at The Maytime Inn, where the garden has a giant Jenga set and a petting zone for resident alpacas.

Day 2: Wildlife Wonder:

- Morning: Cotswold Wildlife Park. Don't miss the new 2025 "Madagascar Zone," where kids can walk through a lemur canopy trail.
- Afternoon: Cotswold Farm Park (Adam Henson's HQ). Time your visit for the 2 PM lamb bottle-feeding session.
- Evening: Movie Night at The Hollow Bottom pub. They project family films onto a hay bale screen—complete with hot chocolate topped with marshmallows bigger than your fist.

Day 3: Miniature Marvels

- **Morning:** Bourton-on-the-Water Model Village. Challenge the kids to find the tiny "hidden cat" in the 1/9th-scale replica of the village.
- **Afternoon:** Dragonfly Maze at Batsford Arboretum. Solve riddles to reach the stone tower, where a golden dragonfly pendant awaits.
- **Evening:** DIY Pizza Night at The King's Arms (Moreton-in-Marsh). Their outdoor oven lets kids top pizzas with foraged wild garlic.

Day 4: Steam & Screams

- **Morning:** Ride the Gloucestershire Warwickshire Steam Railway. In 2025, new "Driver for a Day" tickets let kids (ages 8+) blow the whistle.
- **Afternoon:** Clearwell Caves. Navigate iron-mining tunnels with helmets and headlamps, then hunt for "fool's gold" in the streams.
- **Evening:** Ghost Walk in Chipping Campden. Guide Nigel's tales of the "Headless Horseman of Hoo Lane" are just spooky enough for tweens.

Day 5: Farewell Frolics

- **Morning:** Blenheim Palace's Hedge Maze. Race to the center, then cool off with lemonade in the butterfly house.
- **Finale:** Let the kids spend their souvenir budget at Cotswold Craftsmen (Stow-on-the-Wold). They'll leave with handmade wooden swords or unicorn hair clips (made from real sheep's wool).

7-Day Cultural Deep Dive: Shakespearean Plays and Georgian Architecture.

For those who want to time-travel through England's artistic soul.

Day 1: Arrival in Stratford-upon-Avon

- **Stay:** The Arden Hotel, overlooking the Royal Shakespeare Theatre. Request Room 303—it has a

- balcony where you can eavesdrop on actors rehearsing in the courtyard.
- **Evening:** Julius Caesar at the Swan Theatre. Post-show, debate Brutus' motives over smoked eel pâté at The Opposition.

Day 2: Literary Landscapes

- **Morning:** Shakespeare's Birthplace. Join the 2025 "Sonnet Writing Workshop" in the garden.
- **Afternoon:** Drive to Chipping Campden. Walk the Cotswold Way to Broad Campden, passing the thatched cottage where J.R.R. Tolkien wrote parts of The Hobbit.
- **Evening:** High Tea at Badgers Hall, served on mismatched Wedgwood china. Ask owner Margaret about her great-aunt's affair with a Bloomsbury Group poet.

Day 3: Georgian Grandeur

- **Morning:** Bath Day Trip, Tour the Royal Crescent with Blue Badge guide Sarah, who'll reveal how Georgian ladies hid love letters in their wig poufs.
- **Afternoon:** Fashion Museum, try on replica 18th-century corsets and take selfies in the "Dandy's Den."
- **Evening:** Thermae Bath Spa. Soak in the rooftop pool as the sun dips behind Bath Abbey.

Day 4: Medieval Mystique

- **Morning:** Tewkesbury Abbey, Climb the tower for views of the 1471 Battle of Tewkesbury site.

- **Afternoon:** Sudeley Castle, don't miss the new 2025 exhibition on Katherine Parr's herbal remedies.
- Evening: Medieval Banquet at Stokesay Castle. Eat roast boar with your hands while minstrels play the lute.

Day 5: Arts & Crafts Immersion

- **Morning:** Court Barn Museum (Chipping Campden). Try silver-smithing in their 2025 "Arts & Crafts Revival" workshop.
- **Afternoon:** Hidcote Manor Garden, Sketch the Red Borders, then debate color theory over rhubarb gin in the café.
- **Evening:** Chipping Norton Theatre, catch a avant-garde play in this intimate venue once frequented by Laurence Olivier.

Day 6: Roman Roots

- **Morning:** Cirencester's Corinium Museum, Handle replica Roman coins minted with your face (yes, really).
- **Afternoon:** Chedworth Roman Villa, Join the "Mosaic Masterclass" to lay your own tile in the 2025 community artwork.
- **Evening:** The King's Head (Cirencester). Sip Mulsum (honeyed wine) by the fire and discuss whether Roman Britons preferred oysters or dormice.

Day 7: Farewell to the Muse

- **Morning:** Bibury's St. Mary's Church, play "spot the Green Man" carvings among the pews.

- **Finale:** Sunset at Dover's Hill. Stand where 17th-century poets held Olympic-style games, then read a verse you've written into the wind.

Photography Tour: Golden Hour at Broadway Tower, Lavender Fields at Snowshill.

For those who see the world through lenses and light.

Day 1: Arrival in Broadway

- **Stay:** Russell's of Broadway—rooms have vintage Rolleiflex cameras as décor and blackout curtains for pre-dawn risers.
- **Golden Hour:** Shoot Broadway Tower from Fish Hill. Use a circular polarizer to deepen the sky's blush as sheep graze the foreground.

Day 2: Lavender Dreams

- **Dawn:** Snowshill Lavender Fields (July only). Arrive by 4:30 AM to capture mist weaving through rows of purple. Pro tip: A 70-200mm lens compresses the rows into geometric perfection.
- **Afternoon:** Snowshill Manor Focus on textures—rusty armor against honey stone, sunbeams piercing dusty attic windows.
- **Evening:** Blue Hour in Chipping Campden, Tripod shots of the Market Hall's arches, lit only by a lone lamplighter's torch.

Day 3: Water & Wool

- **Morning:** Lower Slaughter Mill, Long exposures blur the waterwheel into silk, Chat with miller Tom for access to the loft's cobwebbed windows.
- **Afternoon:** Filkins' Cotswold Woollen Weavers, Capture warp and weft in motion, then buy a tweed scarf as a lens cloth.
- **Evening:** Astrophotography at Bredon Hill, New 2025 "Dark Sky Permits" allow after-hours access. The Andromeda Galaxy looks stunning over Saxon burial mounds.

Day 4: Final Frames

- **Morning:** Bibury's Arlington Row Bypass crowds by wading into the River Coln for a reflection shot. Waterproof boots essential!
- **Finale:** Sunset Workshop with pro photographer Claire Davies Her "Cotswolds Light Masterclass" (bookable via Airbnb Experiences) teaches you to chase the "golden ten minutes" when the stone glows like embers.

A Parting Snap

The Cotswolds taught me that the best itineraries aren't etched in stone—they're written in honeyed light, laughter echoing down lanes, and the soft click of a shutter capturing a moment you'll carry forever. So whether you're here to rekindle, explore, or simply see anew, remember: these hills have been waiting for you. Now go—your story's next chapter starts here.

CHAPTER FOUR

Accommodation Guide

Picture this: You've spent the day wandering honey-colored villages, your boots dusty from footpaths lined with cow parsley. Now, the sun dips behind the hills, and you're craving a hot bath, a soft bed, and maybe a pint by a crackling fire. The Cotswolds doesn't just offer a place to sleep—it invites you to live inside its history, luxury, and whimsy. Let's find your perfect nest.

Lodging Styles

Historic Coaching Inns: Sleep Where Shakespeare Did

The scent of aged oak beams, the creak of floorboards trodden by Tudor traders, and the warmth of a log fire that's burned for 500 winters.

The Lygon Arms

- **Address:** Broadway WR12 7DT, United Kingdom
- **Website:** www.lygonarms.co.uk
- **Contact:** +44 1386 852255
- **Price:** £250–£600/night

The Lygon Arm

SCAN THE QR CODE BELOW

1. Open Your Camera or QR Code Scanner App
2. Point Your Camera at the QR Code
3. Wait for the QR Code to be Recognized
4. Tap the Notification or Link
5. View the Map

Why Stay: Charles I holed up here during the Civil War; today, you'll find four-poster beds and a spa in the old wine cellar. Ask for Room 22—Oliver Cromwell allegedly left a ghostly draft in his wake.

The Porch House (England's Oldest Inn!)

- **Address:** 1-3 Digbeth St, Stow-on-the-Wold GL54 1BN.
- **Website:** www.porch-house.co.uk.
- **Contact:** +44 1451 870048.
- **Price:** £180–£400/night

Why Stay: Dating to 947 AD, its low ceilings and stone hearths feel like a hug from history. The **Mulled Wine Croft** room has a freestanding tub overlooking the village square.

Boutique Hotels: 2025's Fresh Faces

Think geometric wallpapers inspired by Arts & Crafts motifs, locally distilled gin minibars, and rooftop terraces strung with fairy lights.

The Painswick (New 2025 Extension!)

- **Address:** Kemps Lane, Painswick GL6 6YB.
- **Website:** www.thepainswick.co.uk.
- **Contact:** +44 1452 813688.
- **Price:** £300–£700/night.

Why Stay: Their new "Artist's Loft" suites include easels and plein air painting kits. Dine in the **Orangery** where dishes like lavender-crusted lamb are paired with Cotswolds Distillery gins.

No. 38 The Park (Cheltenham's Chic Newcomer)

- **Address:** 38 Evesham Rd, Cheltenham GL52 2AH.
- **Website:** www.no38thepark.com.
- **Contact:** +44 1242 370415.
- **Price:** £220–£450/night.

Why Stay: A Georgian townhouse revamped with emerald velvet sofas and curated bookshelves. The Secret Garden Suite opens onto a private patio where breakfast arrives in a wicker hamper.

Quaint B&Bs and Dog-Friendly Cottages.

The aroma of sourdough toasting, the patter of paws on flagstones, and the thrill of finding a vintage rotary phone in your room.

The Old Stocks Inn (Dog-Friendly!)

- **Address:** The Square, Stow-on-the-Wold GL54 1AF.
- **Website:** www.oldstocksinn.com.
- **Contact:** +44 1451 830666.
- **Price:** £120–£300/night .

The Old Stocks Inn

SCAN THE QR CODE BELOW

1. Open Your Camera or QR Code Scanner App
2. Point Your Camera at the QR Code
3. Wait for the QR Code to be Recognized
4. Tap the Notification or Link
5. View the Map

Why Stay: Dogs get their own hamper (organic treats, a chew toy). The Garden Rooms have private patios perfect for post-walk muddy paws.

Broadway Cottage (Self-Catering Charm)

- **Address:** 45 High St, Broadway WR12 7DP.
- **Website:** www.broadway-cottages.co.uk.
- **Contact:** +44 1386 852937.
- **Price:** £150–£350/night (3-night min).

Why Stay: A 17th-century weaver's cottage with an AGA stove and a sun trap garden. The owner leaves a welcome pack of local bacon and duck eggs.

Eco-Glamping and Solar-Powered Farm Stay.

The rustle of canvas in the breeze, the earthy smell of composting toilets done right, and the taste of campfire-roasted marshmallows.

Luxury Cotswold Camping

- **Address:** Fosseway, Moreton-in-Marsh GL56 9NQ.
- **Website:** www.luxurycotswoldcamping.co.uk.
- **Contact:** +44 1608 238533.
- **Price:** £120–£250/night

Why Stay: Their 2025 "Sky Domes" have retractable roofs for stargazing and solar-powered underfloor heating. Borrow a fire pit kit for sunset s'mores.

50 | Cotswolds Travel Guide 2025

Green Acres Farm Stay

- **Address:** Green Acres Ln, Blockley GL56 9EX.
- **Website:** www.greenacresfarmstay.co.uk.
- **Contact:** +44 1386 700432.
- **Price:** £90–£180/night

Why Stay: Help collect eggs at dawn or bike to nearby Batsford Arboretum. The Shepherd's Hut runs entirely on solar power and has a wood-fired hot tub.

Chipping Campden: Gateway to the Cotswold Way.

The crunch of gravel underfoot on the High Street, the tang of artisan cheese from the Saturday market, and the distant clang of the blacksmith's hammer.

Noel Arms

- **Address:** High St, Chipping Campden GL55 6AT
- **Website:** www.noelarms.co.uk
- **Contact:** +44 1386 840317.
- **Price:** £180–£400).

Why stay: Their Cotswold Way Walker's Package includes packed lunches and boot drying. Don't Miss: Hidcote Manor Garden (a 10-minute drive; pre-book timed tickets online).

Cheltenham: Regency Elegance and Festival Hub.

The hum of jazz spilling from festival tents, the clink of champagne at the races, and the swish of silk dresses on Promenade.

The Queens Hotel

- **Address:** The Promenade, Cheltenham GL50 1NN.
- **Website:** www.thequeenshotelcheltenham.co.uk
- **Contact:** +44 1242 515699.
- **Price:** £220-£500.

Why Stay: The Festival Suite has a balcony overlooking the Literary Festival tents. Don't Miss Montpellier Wine Bar for people-watching and local ciders.

Tetbury: Royal Connections and Antique Treasures.

The musk of aged wood in antique shops, the sweet scent of Highgrove roses, and the murmur of royal gossip at the pub.

The Close Hotel

- **Address:** 8 Long St, Tetbury GL8 8AQ
- **Website:** www.theclosehotel.com
- **Contact:** +44 1666 502272.
- **Price:** £160–£350.

Why Stay: The Royal Retreat Room has a four-poster bed fit for Camilla (who's popped in for tea, allegedly). Don't Miss Highgrove Gardens tours (www.highgrovegardens.com).

A Final Tip from Your Cotswolds Confidant.

The secret to nailing your Cotswolds stay? Embrace the quirks. Book the room with the slanting floor. Let the innkeeper's labrador lead you to the breakfast table. And always, always accept the offer of a homemade scone. These hills have been perfecting hospitality for a millennium—trust them to tuck you in right.

Now, go forth and nap in four-poster beds, soak in solar-heated tubs, and dream of sheep-dotted horizons. Your perfect Cotswolds chapter starts here.

CHAPTER FIVE

Iconic Cotswolds Experiences

I magine the golden morning light spilling over honey-stone cottages, the chatter of sheep in distant meadows, and the crunch of gravel underfoot as you step into a storybook. The Cotswolds isn't just a place—it's a living museum, a canvas of rolling hills, and a stage for tales older than Shakespeare. Let's dive into its most iconic treasures, with all the insider tips you'd get from a local friend.

Must-See Villages: Timeless Beauty in Every Cobblestone.

Bibury's Arlington Row

The scent of wild thyme, the soft babble of the River Coln, and cottages glowing like amber in the dawn light.

- **Address:** Arlington Row, Bibury, Cirencester GL7 5N.
- **Website:** www.nationaltrust.org.uk/bibury.
- **Contact:** +44 1285 740249.
- **Entry:** Free (donation suggested); Parking £5/day.

Why Visit: These 17th-century weavers' cottages are the Cotswolds' poster child for a reason. Arrive before 9 AM to photograph the iconic row without crowds. Pop into The

Catherine Wheel pub afterward for a pint of Hooky Ale and their famous sausage rolls (£6).

Insider Tip: Follow the footpath behind the cottages to Bibury Trout Farm (GL7 5NL). Feed the rainbow trout (£2 for a handful of pellets) and pretend you're in a Merchant Ivory film.

Castle Combe: The Prettiest Village in England

The whisper of wind through ancient yew trees, the clop of horse hooves on cobbles, and the faintest whiff of mossy stone.

- **Address:** Castle Combe, Chippenham SN14 7HT.
- **Website:** www.castlecombe.info.
- **Contact:** Village info via Wiltshire Council (+44 1249 706456).
- **Entry: Free:** Parking £4/day at the village car park.

Why Visit: This untouched medieval village has starred in War Horse and Downton Abbey. Don't miss the 14th-century Market Cross or the St. Andrew's Church tombstone etched with a mysterious medieval "doodle" of a dog.

Insider Tip: Dine at The Castle Inn (High St, SN14 7HN). Their afternoon tea (£25) includes scones with clotted cream so thick, you'll swear it's butter.

Historic Estates: Palaces, Castles, and Royal Gardens.

Blenheim Palace: A Baroque Masterpiece

The echo of footsteps on marble floors, the rustle of tapestries, and the sweet tang of Capability Brown's rose gardens.

- **Address:** Woodstock OX20 1UL.
- **Website:** www.blenheimpalace.com.
- **Contact:** +44 1993 810530.
- **Entry:** £35/adult (park and gardens), £49/palace tour.

Why Visit: Birthplace of Winston Churchill, this UNESCO site dazzles with its Vanbrugh-designed halls. Rent a rowboat (£20/hour) on the lake for views of the Grand Bridge.

Insider Tip: Visit the Butterfly House (free with entry) at midday when the sun ignites their wings into stained glass.

Sudeley Castle: Tudor Drama & Secret Gardens

The creak of oak doors, the scent of heritage roses, and the ghostly rustle of Katherine Parr's gown.

- **Address:** Winchcombe GL54 5JD.
- **Website:** www.sudeleycastle.co.uk.
- **Contact:** +44 1242 604244.
- **Entry:** £20/adult (castle and garden).

Why Visit: The only private castle in England with a queen buried in its grounds (Parr, Henry VIII's last wife). The Phoenix Garden's peacocks will photobomb your selfies.

Insider Tip: Grab a cream tea (£12) at the Tudor Café and sit where Elizabeth I once dined.

Highgrove Gardens: The Prince's Passion Project

The hum of bees in wildflower meadows, the earthy scent of organic compost, and the crunch of gravel under royal-approved Wellies.

- **Address:** Doughton, Tetbury GL8 8TN.
- **Website:** www.highgrovegardens.com.
- **Contact:** +44 303 123 7303.
- **Entry:** £32.50/adult (guided tour only; book 3+ months ahead).

SCAN THE QR CODE BELOW

1. Open Your Camera or QR Code Scanner App
2. Point Your Camera at the QR Code
3. Wait for the QR Code to be Recognized
4. Tap the Notification or Link
5. View the Map

Why Visit: King Charles III's organic oasis. The Thyme Walk and Stumpery feel like Narnia meets The Crown.

Insider Tip: Post-tour, shop at Highgrove Shop (10 Long St, Tetbury). Their lavender shortbread (£8) is fit for a coronation.

Gardens & Nature: Blooms, Arboretums, and Wild Wonders.

Hidcote Manor Garden: Arts & Crafts Heaven

The buzz of pollinators in jewel-toned borders, the snap of shears shaping yew hedges, and the tang of homemade lemonade.

- **Address:** Hidcote Bartrim, Chipping Campden GL55 6LR.
- **Website:** www.nationaltrust.org.uk/hidcote.
- **Contact:** +44 1386 438333.
- **Entry:** £15/adult.

Why Visit: Lawrence Johnston's masterpiece, where "garden rooms" explode with color. The Red Borders (best in July) are a photographer's dream.

Insider Tip: The Plant Shop sells rare cuttings—sneak a sprig of Hidcote lavender into your suitcase.

Westonbirt Arboretum: A Symphony of Trees

The rustle of 15,000 leaves, the sharp scent of pine, and the soft thud of acorns hitting forest floors.

- **Address:** Tetbury GL8 8QS.
- **Website:** www.forestryengland.uk/westonbirt.
- **Contact:** +44 300 067 4890.
- **Entry:** £12/adult.

Why Visit: Home to the UK's tallest redwood. The STIHL Treetop Walkway (free with entry) offers canopy-level views. October's fiery maples are unmissable.

Insider Tip: Rent a Balance Bike (£10) for kids—they'll burn energy on the Silk Wood trails while you picnic.

Architectural Gems: From Saxon Simplicity to Wool Church Grandeur.

Northleach's St. Peter & St. Paul: A Wool Church Masterpiece.

The echo of Gregorian chants, the chill of medieval stone, and the glint of sunlight through 15th-century-stained glass.

- **Address:** Market Square, Northleach GL54 3EH.
- **Website:** www.northleach.org.
- **Contact:** +44 1451 860715.
- **Entry:** Free (donation suggested).

Why Visit: Funded by 15th-century wool merchants, this "Cathedral of the Cotswolds" boasts brasses depicting wool sacks. Find the quirky Green Man carving near the pulpit.

Insider Tip: Time your visit with the Thursday Market (9 AM–1 PM) for local cheese and honey.

Odda's Chapel: Saxon Serenity

The whisper of 1,000 years of prayers, the rough texture of Saxon stone, and the quiet creak of a wooden door.

- **Address:** Deerhurst, Gloucester GL19 4BX.
- **Website:** www.english-heritage.org.uk/oddas-chapel).
- **Contact:** +44 370 333 1181.
- **Entry:** Free.

Odda's Chapel

SCAN THE QR CODE BELOW

1. Open Your Camera or QR Code Scanner App
2. Point Your Camera at the QR Code
3. Wait for the QR Code to be Recognized
4. Tap the Notification or Link
5. View the Map

Why Visit: Built in 1056, this tiny chapel is one of England's oldest intact buildings. The simple stone altar feels humbling.

Insider Tip: Pair with a visit to The Farmers Arms (Deerhurst GL19 4BX) for cider and tales of the chapel's Viking-era origins.

2025 Highlights: New Reasons to Fall in Love.
Snowshill Manor: Eccentricity Unleashed

The clatter of 22,000 curiosities, the lavender-scented breeze from the fields, and the creak of a 17th-century rocking horse.

- **Address:** Snowshill, Broadway WR12 7JU.
- **Website:** www.nationaltrust.org.uk/snowshill-manor).

- **Contact:** +44 1386 852410.
- **Entry:** £14/adult.

Why Visit: This madcap manor houses a taxidermized cat in a dollhouse and a room full of bicycles. The Lavender Fields (July bloom) are Instagram gold.

Insider Tip: The Manor Tea Room serves lavender ice cream (£3.50)—eat it while pondering Wade's obsession with the color blue.

Broadway Tower: Renovated Views

The whistle of wind through Cotswold stone, the distant bleat of sheep, and the click of a thousand camera shutters.

- **Address:** Middle Hill, Broadway WR12 7LB.
- **Website:** www.broadwaytower.co.uk.
- **Contact:** +44 1386 852390.
- **Entry:** £8/adult (tower access).

Why Visit: Climb the 65 steps for views stretching to Wales. Spot Bredon Hill's ancient burial mounds.

Insider Tip: Visit at sunset and join the Tower Twilight Tour (£15)—they'll hand you a blanket and a flask of hot chocolate.

A Final Word from Your Cotswolds Companion.

The Cotswolds isn't about ticking boxes—it's about letting the landscape seep into your soul. Whether you're marveling at a Saxon chapel or giggling at Snowshill's oddities, remember: these places have survived plagues, wars, and Instagram. Treat them gently, linger longer than planned, and always save room for cake.

Now, lace up your boots, charge your camera, and let's make memories that'll outlast even the oldest yew tree.

CHAPTER SIX

Cultural Experiences

Close your eyes and listen: the clink of a potter's wheel in a sunlit studio, the roar of a crowd cheering on wool-sack racers, and the hush of a theater as the curtain rises. The Cotswolds isn't just about postcard views—it's a living, breathing tapestry of creativity and heritage. Let's dive into its cultural heart, one immersive experience at a time.

Museums: Time Travel Through Artifacts and Craft.

Corinium Museum: Roman Riches Under Your Feet

The cool whisper of ancient stone, the gleam of gold coins under glass, and the musty scent of history preserved.

- **Address:** Park St, Cirencester GL7 2BX.
- **Website:** www.coriniummuseum.org.
- **Contact:** +44 1285 655611.
- **Entry:** £8.50/adult, £4/child (Family ticket £20).

<u>Why Visit:</u> This award-winning museum houses Britain's finest Roman artifacts outside London. Don't miss the 2025 exhibit Legion: Life in the Roman Army, featuring a reconstructed soldier's barracks and interactive sandal-making workshops.

Personal Moment: I once spent an hour here chatting with a volunteer about how Romans flavored their wine with garum (fermented fish sauce). Spoiler: It's better left in the past.

Church Barn Museum: Where Arts & Crafts Thrive.

The hum of a jeweler's saw, the earthy smell of fresh clay, and the soft rustle of archival sketches.

- **Address:** Church St, Chipping Campden GL55 6JE.
- **Website:** www.courtbarn.org.uk.
- **Contact:** +44 1386 841951.
- **Entry:** £6/adult, Under 16s free.

Why Visit: Celebrates the Cotswolds' craft revival with displays on silversmiths, bookbinders, and the Guild of Handicraft. The 2025 spotlight is on Katharine Adams, a trailblazing Arts & Crafts bookbinder.

Insider Tip: Book a Silver Ring Workshop (£65, 2 hours) to forge your own jewelry under a master silversmith's eye.

Festivals: Celebrate Like a Local.

Cheltenham Literature Festival: Wordsmith Wonderland

The crisp rustle of book pages, the buzz of heated literary debates, and the aroma of espresso from pop-up cafés.

- **Dates:** October 3-12, 2025.
- **Location:** Montpellier Gardens, Cheltenham GL50 1SD.
- **Website:** www.cheltenhamfestivals.com/literature.
- **Contact:** +44 1242 850270.
- **Tickets:** £10-£35 per event; Early bird passes from £150.

Winchcombe Pottery: Spin, Shape, and Glaze

The gritty slip of wet clay between fingers, the rhythmic whir of the wheel, and the tang of kiln-fired minerals.

- **Address:** Abbey Terrace, Winchcombe GL54 5PJ.
- **Website:** www.winchcombepottery.co.uk.
- **Contact:** +44 1242 604321.

- **Workshop:** 2-Hour Throw & Glaze (£55/person).

Why Visit: Learn from third-generation potter Tom Green, whose mugs grace Cotswold breakfast tables. Take home a piece fired in their wood-burning kiln.

Insider Tip: Book the Sunset Session (6–8 PM). Sipping local cider while crafting is pure magic.

Dry Stone Walling Demos: Building Like the Ancients

The clack of limestone finding its place, the crunch of gravel under boots, and the instructor's patient "Nudge it left, lad."

- **Location:** Various sites; book via Cotswolds Conservation Board.

- **Website:** www.cotswoldsaonb.org.uk.
- **Contact:** +44 1451 862000.
- **Workshop:** Half-Day Intro (£40; includes tools and tea)

Why Visit: Master a 5,000-year-old craft. The 2025 Great Wall Build-Off (Sept 20) lets teams compete to repair historic boundaries.

Performing Arts: Curtain Up in the Countryside.

Everyman Theatre Cheltenham:

Regency Glamour Meets Modern Drama. The velvet rustle of seats, the anticipatory hush before Act I, and the citrusy zing of pre-show G&Ts.

- **Address:** Regent St, Cheltenham GL50 1HQ.
- **Website:** everymantheatre.org.uk).
- **Contact:** +44 1242 572573.
- **Tickets:** £20–£60; Student rush seats £15 (30 mins before show).

Insider Tip: Backstage tours (£12) reveal ghost stories about the "Lady in Grey" who haunts the dressing rooms.

Chipping Norton Theatre: Intimate and Inventive

The creak of a 19th-century stage, the warmth of a pre-show mulled wine, and the collective gasp at a plot twist.

- **Address:** 2 Spring St, Chipping Norton OX7 5NL.
- **Website:** www.chippingnortontheatre.com.
- **Contact:** +44 1608 642350.
- **Tickets:** £15–£35

Insider Tip: Post-show, head to The Chequers pub. Actors often linger for a debrief over pork pies.

A Cultural Curtain Call

The Cotswolds' culture isn't locked in glass cases—it's in the mud on your boots after a walling workshop, the ink smudges from a signed novel, and the shared laughter of a theater crowd. So, whether you're molding clay in Winchcombe or debating Dickens over a pint, remember: here, every experience is a story waiting to be lived.

Now, go scribble your own chapter in this ancient, ever-evolving tale.

CHAPTER SEVEN

Culinary Adventures

Close your eyes and inhale: the earthy aroma of freshly baked sourdough, the tang of cider fermenting in oak barrels, and the sweet perfume of lavender shortbread cooling on a farmhouse windowsill. The Cotswolds isn't just a feast for the eyes—it's a banquet for the senses. From clinking pub pints with shepherds to sipping gin distilled from meadow flowers, let's dig into the flavors that define this land.

Farm-to-Table: Soil to Soul Dining

Daylesford Organic: The Gold Standard of Green

The crunch of gravel underfoot, the hum of bees in the herb garden, and the warm waft of wood-fired sourdough.

- **Address:** Daylesford, Kingham, Chipping Norton GL56 0YG.
- **Website:** www.daylesford.com.
- **Contact:** +44 1608 731700.
- **Price:** Café mains £15-£30; Farm Shop groceries from £5.

Dalesford Organic

SCAN THE QR CODE BELOW

1. Open Your Camera or QR Code Scanner App
2. Point Your Camera at the QR Code
3. Wait for the QR Code to be Recognized
4. Tap the Notification or Link
5. View the Map

<u>Why Visit:</u> This 2,500-acre organic haven is a foodie pilgrimage. Their 2025 Spring Menu features wild garlic pesto made from foraged greens and lamb reared on clover-rich pastures. Don't miss the Cookery School (£120/class)—I once burned a rosemary focaccia here, but the instructors still hugged me.

<u>Insider Tip:</u> Grab a Farmer's Lunchbox (£12) from the deli and picnic by the alpaca paddock.

Diddly Squat Farm Shop: Clarkson's Controversial Gem

The clatter of Hawkstone lager bottles, the earthy musk of "Gerald" the tractor, and the occasional grumble from Jeremy himself.

- **Address:** Chipping Norton Rd, Chadlington OX7 3PE.
- **Website:** www.diddlysquad.com.
- **Contact:** No phone—just turn up and hope he's not filming!
- **Price:** Farm shop items £3–£20; Bee Juice (honey) is a steal at £8.

Why Visit: Love him or loathe him, Clarkson's farm shop is a cultural artifact. The 2025 "Lambing Live" weekends (Feb-Mar) let you cuddle newborn lambs while sipping his Gin in a Tin (£5).

Insider Tip: Visit on a weekday afternoon to avoid Grand Tour fan mobs.

Local Flavors: Taste Centuries of Tradition
Double Gloucester Cheese: A Golden Legacy

The creamy tang of unpasteurized milk, the crinkle of waxed paper, and the smug satisfaction of out-cheesing your Instagram followers.

- **Address:** (The Cotswold Cheese Company) 4-5 Stow Rd, Moreton-in-Marsh GL56 0AD
- **Website:** www.cotswoldcheesecompany.co.uk
- **Contact:** +44 1608 652862
- **Price:** Their Smoked Double Gloucester (£6/200g) is life-changing.

Highlight: St. James Cheese Stall (Stroud Farmers' Market): Saturdays 9 AM–2 PM. Chat with cheesemaker Tom—he'll let you sample cheese aged in local cider casks.

Tewkesbury Mustard: Medieval Heat

The sinus-clearing zing of horseradish, the earthy sweetness of apple cider vinegar, and the faint echo of Henry VIII's belches.

- **Address:** (The Tewkesbury Mustard Shop) 64 Church St, Tewkesbury GL20 5RZ.
- **Website:** www.tewkesburymustard.co.uk.
- **Contact:** +44 1684 292322.

- **Price:** The Original Sin blend (£4.50/jar) pairs perfectly with a Sunday roast.

Pubs & Dining: From Ancient Alehouses to Michelin Stars.

The Wild Rabbit: Where Rustic Meets Refined

The crackle of a log fire, the murmur of wellies on flagstones, and the pop of a natural wine cork.

- **Address:** Church St, Kingham, Chipping Norton OX7 6YA.
- **Website:** www.thewildrabbit.co.uk.
- **Contact:** +44 1608 658389.
- **Price:** Mains £25–£40; Sunday roast £35.

Why Visit: Michelin-starred chef Nathan Eades helms the kitchen. The Hay-Smoked Venison (sourced from the Daylesford estate) is a masterpiece.

Insider Tip: Book the Snug for intimate dinners—it's a 17th-century priest hole with candlelit charm.

The Porch House: England's Oldest Inn

The creak of 1,078-year-old floorboards, the yeasty froth of a cask ale, and the sizzle of sausages from pigs named Kevin and Dave.

- **Address:** 1-3 Digbeth St, Stow-on-the-Wold GL54 1BN.

- **Website:** www.porch-house.co.uk.
- **Contact:** +44 1451 870048.
- **Price:** Mains £16-£28; Ale £5/pint.

Why Visit: Built in 94 AD, this pub serves Braised Cotswold Lamb in a room where Crusaders once drank. The Churchill Ale (brewed next door) is a malty marvel.

Insider Tip: Ask for the Secret Menu—locals know to request the off-menu Ploughman's Platter for Two (£30), piled with pork pies and piccalilli.

Tours: Sip, Swirl, and Savor.

Cotswolds Distillery: Gin with a View

The junipery bite of small-batch spirits, the clink of tasting glasses, and the hum of bees polluting the botanicals.

- **Address:** Phillips Field, Whichford, Shipston-on-Stour CV36 5EX.
- **Website:** www.cotswoldsdistillery.com.
- **Contact:** +44 1608 238533.
- **Tours:** £25/person (includes 4 tastings); 2025 Exclusive Honeybee Gin Experience (£45), blending your own gin with apiary-fresh honey.

Why Visit: Their Dry Gin No. 90 won World's Best in 2024. The distillery cats, Barley and Hops, are bonus fluffballs.

Hook Norton Brewery: Victorian Ale Alchemy

The malty steam rising from copper kettles, the clatter of dray carts on cobbles, and the yeasty burp of fermentation.

- **Address:** Brewery Ln, Hook Norton, Banbury OX15 5NY.
- **Website:** www.hooky.co.uk.
- **Contact:** +44 1608 730384.
- **Tours:** £18/person (includes 3 half-pints).

Why Visit: This family-run brewery still uses a 25-horsepower steam engine. The Old Hooky ale is like liquid caramel.

Insider Tip: Time your visit with the Brewery Beer Festival (June 14–16, 2025) for live folk music and rare cask tipples.

A Final Toast from Your Culinary Guide

The Cotswolds taught me that food isn't just fuel—it's a language. It's the farmer who hands you a still-warm apple with dirt under his nails. It's the pub landlord who remembers how you take your pint. It's the gin that tastes like summer meadows because, well, it's *made* from them. So, loosen your belt, raise a glass, and let every bite and sip whisper the stories of this land.

Now, go forth and eat like every meal's a chapter in your own Cotswolds epic.

CHAPTER EIGHT

Shopping And Local Crafts

Picture this: You're standing in a sunlit studio, watching molten glass twist into a vase as a craftsman hums a folk tune. Outside, the breeze carries the earthy scent of wool fresh off the loom. The Cotswolds isn't just a place to shop—it's a living gallery of artisans, antiques, and traditions passed down through generations. Let's explore its treasures, from amber jewels to sheep's wool spun into gold.

Antique Havens: Treasures with Tales

Fosse Gallery Fine Art (Stow-on-the-Wold

The soft creak of oak floorboards, the gleam of gilt frames, and the hush of a gallery where even the dust feels culture.

- **Address:** 12 Talbot Court, Stow-on-the-Wold GL54 1BZ.
- **Website:** www.fossegallery.com.
- **Contact:** +44 1451 831319.
- **Price Range:** £500–£20,000 (Yes, that's a small David Hockney sketch in the corner).

Fosse Gallery

SCAN THE QR CODE BELOW

1. Open Your Camera or QR Code Scanner App
2. Point Your Camera at the QR Code
3. Wait for the QR Code to be Recognized
4. Tap the Notification or Link
5. View the Map

Why Visit: This boutique gallery showcases contemporary Cotswolds artists. The 2025 "Landscapes in Light" exhibit features ethereal oil paintings of the Windrush Valley.

Insider Tip: Chat with owner Rosemary—she'll share stories of artists who've sipped tea in the back room, including a tipsy Lucian Freud anecdote.

Long Street Antiques (Tetbury)

The tick of a grandfather clock, the musky aroma of aged leather, and the thrill of spotting a 17th-century map of Gloucestershire.

- **Address:** 10 Long St, Tetbury GL8 8AQ.
- **Website:** www.longstreetantiques.co.uk.
- **Contact:** +44 1666 50434.

- **Price Range:** £50 (vintage spoons) to £15,000 (Regency mahogany escritoire)

Why Visit: A labyrinth of 30+ dealers under one roof. Don't miss Lorfords Antiques' collection of whimsical taxidermy (think monocled owls).

Artisan Markets: Where Locals Stock Their Larders.

Cirencester Charter Market (Saturdays)

The clatter of cheese wires slicing Double Gloucester, the tang of fresh-pressed apple juice, and the banter of farmers in tweed caps.

- **Address:** Market Place, Cirencester GL7 2NY.
- **Hours:** Every Saturday, 9 AM–3 PM (rain or shine!).
- **Website:** www.cirencester.gov.uk/market.

SCAN THE QR CODE BELOW
1. Open Your Camera or QR Code Scanner App
2. Point Your Camera at the QR Code
3. Wait for the QR Code to be Recognized
4. Tap the Notification or Link
5. View the Map

Must-Buy: Bath Pig's chorizo scotch eggs (£4 each). Grab a baguette from Hobbs House Bakery and build a picnic on the spot.

Insider Tip: Arrive by 9:30 AM for The Cotswold Cure's wild boar salami—it sells out fast.

Moreton-in-Marsh Tuesday Market

The rustle of hessian sacks, the sweet perfume of just-picked strawberries, and the jingle of a toy train circling a wooden stall.

- **Address:** High St, Moreton-in-Marsh GL56 0AF.
- **Hours:** Tuesdays, 8 AM–3 PM.
- **Website:** www.moreton-in-marsh.co.uk/market).

Must-Buy: Cotswold Cheese Company's nettle-wrapped cheese (£8.50). Pair with The Cotswold Distillery's damson gin (£28) from the adjacent stall.

Insider Tip: Park at the Redesdale Hall car park (£2 all day)—it's a 2-minute walk and avoids High Street chaos.

Wool Heritage: From Fleece to Fashion.
Filkins' Traditional Weavers.

The rhythmic clack of the loom, the lanolin-rich smell of raw fleece, and the soft snip of shears trimming tweed.

- **Address:** 3 Filkins, Lechlade GL7 3JQ.
- **Website:** www.filkinsweavers.co.uk.
- **Contact:** +44 1367 860618.
- **Price Range:** £30 (wool blankets) to £250 (bespoke tweed jackets).

Why Visit: One of England's last working wool mills. Their 2025 "Heritage Tweed" line uses natural dyes from woad and madder root.

Insider Tip: Demo days (first Saturday monthly) let you try weaving—expect to leave with thread in your hair.

Cold Aston Mill

The rumble of the waterwheel, the thump of felt being pressed, and the cozy weight of a sheepskin rug in your arms.

- **Address:** Cold Aston, Cheltenham GL54 3BN.
- **Website:** www.coldastonmill.co.uk.
- **Contact:** +44 1451 821325.
- **Price Range:** £20 (lambswool socks) to £400 (hand-tufted rugs).

Why Visit: This 18th-century mill now creates sustainable homewares. The Mill Shop sells "imperfect" knitwear at a steal—my £50 chunky cardigan is a winter staple.

A Final Word from Your Shopping Sherpa

Shopping here isn't transactional—it's conversational. It's the weaver who explains how her great-grandmother carded wool in the same barn. It's the glassblower who lets your toddler "help" blow a bubble (true story—my niece's lopsided ornament is priceless). So, slow down, ask questions, and remember: every purchase supports a story that's been unfolding for centuries.

Now, grab your reusable tote and let's hunt for treasures. That hand-thrown mug or amber pendant? It's not just a souvenir—it's a piece of the Cotswolds' soul.

CHAPTER NINE

Practical Information

Let me tell you about the time I got lost near Slad at dusk, my phone dead, mist rolling in like a scene from Wuthering Heights. A farmer found me, handed me a torch, and said, "Them footpaths'll lead you home—just follow the sheep tracks." That's the Cotswolds: a place where preparedness meets serendipity. Here's everything you need to navigate these hills like a local, from emergency contacts to decoding dialect.

Emergencies: Staying Safe in the Slow Lane

NHS Walk-In Clinics & Rural Pharmacies

The sterile tang of antiseptic, the soft bleep of a waiting room monitors, and the relief of a friendly nurse handing you blister plasters for blistered feet.

Cirencester Hospital Minor Injury Unit:

- **Address:** Tetbury Rd, Cirencester GL7 1UY.
- **Hours:** 8 AM–8 PM daily.
- **Contact:** +44 0300 421 7777.

Tips: For sprains or cuts, they're faster than A&E. I once got a sprained ankle wrapped here in 20 minutes.

Stow Pharmacy:

- **Address:** 4 Talbot Court, Stow-on-the-Wold GL54 1BZ.
- **Hours:** 9 AM–6 PM (closed Sundays).
- **Contact:** +44 1451 830341

Must-Have: Their "Hiker's First Aid Kit" (£12) includes Compeed, antihistamines, and a whistle for sheep-related emergencies (yes, really).

After-Hours Help: Dial 111 for non-life-threatening issues. In remote areas, postcode GL56 0XX (Bourton Health Centre) has a 24/7 call button.

Accessibility: Exploring Without Limits

Adapted Trails & Accessible Attractions

The smooth roll of a wheelchair on compacted gravel, the chirp of a trail audio guide, and the scent of wild thyme at nose level.

Broadway Tower:

- **Ramped Access:** Yes (except tower summit).
- **Sensory Guide:** Free tactile maps with Braille descriptions.

Cotswold Farm Park:

- **All-Terrain Wheelchairs:** Free to borrow (book ahead: +44 1451 850307).
- **Accessible Petting Zones:** Raised platforms for stroking pygmy goats.

Sudeley Castle:

- **Mobility Scooter Hire:** £15/day. The Phoenix Garden's paths are cobble-free.
- **Top Trail:** Chedworth Roman Villa's Roman Way (1.2 miles, firm gravel). Rest stops with bench-height artifact replicas.

Safety: Cotswolds Commonsense.

Livestock Etiquette

- The "baa "of curious sheep, the "clang" of a gate closing, and the squelch of wellies avoiding cowpats.
- **Cows:** Walk calmly, no sudden moves. If calves are present, detour widely.
- **Sheep:** Don't feed them—they'll mob you for Jelly Babies (learnt the hard way).
- **Horses:** Approach from the side, speak softly. They're used to riders, not selfie sticks.

Night Navigation:

- **Essential Gear:** A headlamp (Petzl Actik Core, £65) and Ordnance Survey Map OL45.
- **Guided Night Walks:** Cotswolds Outdoor (+44 1451 843123) runs full-moon hikes (£20pp) with stargazing pit stops.

Local Lingo: Cotswolds Dictionary

The twinkle in a farmer's eye as you say "gurt lush," the baffled smile when you call a stream a "brook."

- **"Gurt":** Very ("That's a gurt big hill!").
- **"Lush":** Lovely ("Them scones are proper lush").
- **"Twitten":** A narrow alley (Saxon term still used in Painswick).
- **"Dreckly":** Eventually ("The bus'll come dreckly").

Phrase to Master: "Where's the knackering house?" = Public toilet. Use in Stow's Square for instant local cred.

Transport Timetables: 2025 Updates.
Buses & Trains

The rattle of a vintage timetable pinned to a village noticeboard, the ding of a contactless card on a bus reader.

Key Changes:

- **Pulhams 801 (Cheltenham–Bourton):** New Sunday service! 9 AM–6 PM, hourly.
- **GWR Trains (London Paddington–Moreton-in-Marsh):** Faster 2025 "Cotswold Flyer" (1h15m journey).

Real-Time Apps:

- **Cotswolds Rider:** Tracks buses via QR codes at stops.
- **Trainline:** Now integrates EV hire bikes at stations.

Pro Tip: National Express 444 (London–Cheltenham) now has USB-C ports and free Cotswolds audio guides.

Ethical Viewing: Stay on paths, no picking. Farmers will side-eye tramplers.

A Parting Word from Your Cotswolds Confidant.

The secret to thriving here? Slow down. Let the sheep cross first. Pause to chat with the postmistress. Pack a spare battery and a paper map. These hills have cradled wayfarers for centuries—they'll guide you too, if you let them. Now, go make memories (and maybe feed a lamb). I'll be here, sipping a Hooky Ale at The Porch House, ready to toast your adventures.

CONCLUSION

Where Time Lingers and Footprints

Fade

P icture this: You're sitting on a weathered stone stile near the Slad Valley, a half-eaten pork pie in one hand and a dog-eared map in the other. The sun dips below the horizon, painting the hills in shades of burnt orange and lavender. A farmer ambles by, tipping his cap as his sheep shuffle home. Your phone has been dead for hours, but you don't care—because here, in this moment, you've discovered the Cotswolds' greatest secret: slow travel isn't a trend; it's a homecoming.

Parting Thoughts: Embracing Slow Travel in a Fast-Paced World.

When I first came to the Cotswolds, I raced through villages like a checklist warrior—Bibury by 9 AM, Bourton by noon, Stow by tea time. It wasn't until I got lost near Naunton that I understood what I'd been missing. My map had blown into a ditch, my phone battery drowned in a rainstorm, and I found myself stranded at a farm gate. An elderly woman named Mabel invited me into her kitchen for **"a proper cuppa,"** and as we sat by her AGA stove, she told me about the Bronze Age burial mound behind her barn. **"Nobody visits that old heap,"** she said, **"but it's seen more sunrises than you and I ever will."**

That's the magic of slow travel here. It's trading the rush for the rustle of wind through barley. It's letting a 4-mile hike stretch into 6 because you stopped to chat with a beekeeper. It's realizing that the "must-see" attraction isn't Blenheim Palace—it's the way the light slants through your B&B window at golden hour, or the shopkeeper who remembers how you take your coffee.

Your Role in Preservation: Leaving Light Footprints for Future Generations.

The Cotswolds has survived plagues, wars, and the invention of the selfie stick. But today, its greatest threat is love—the kind that arrives in coachloads, tramples bluebell woods for Instagram, and mistakes drystone walls for climbing frames. Preservation here isn't about rules; it's about respect. Here's how to love these hills without leaving scars:

Shop Like a Local, not a Tourist

- ✓ **Skip the Plastic "Cotswolds" Tat:** Buy a jar of Honeybourne Preserves (made in Stow) or a Filkins Wool Throw instead.
- ✓ **Farmers' Markets > Gift Shops:** The £5 you spend on Stroud Tomatoes keeps a fifth-generation grower afloat.

Walk Softly (Literally)

- ✓ **Stay on Marked Paths:** Those "shortcuts" through fields? They're crushing skylark nests. Use Cotswold Wardens' Apps for approved routes.

- ✓ **Leave Gates as You Find Them:** If it's open, leave it open. If it's closed, "leave it closed". Farmers aren't being rude—they're keeping sheep from motorways.

Dine Responsibly

- ✓ **Choose Pubs with "Slow Food" Certifications:** The Kingham Plough sources 90% of ingredients within 15 miles.
- ✓ **Avoid Peak Times:** Lunch at 2 PM means you'll savor your **Wild Rabbit pie** without elbowing coach tourists.

Be a Wildlife Whisperer

- ✓ **Otters Need Quiet:** If you spot one on the Coln, put the camera down. Your silence lets them teach cubs to fish.
- ✓ **Orchids Aren't Selfie Props:** Kneel, admire, but never pick. (Fun fact: Some species take 15 years to bloom once.)

Honor the Human Heritage

- ✓ **Chat. Listen. Repeat.:** Ask the Broadway Tower custodian about the time she met Judi Dench. Let the Chipping Campden blacksmith rant about coal prices. These stories are the Cotswolds' heartbeat.
- ✓ **Volunteer a Morning:** Join a Drystone Walling Workshop or a Churchyard Clean-Up. You'll leave with dirty nails and a full heart.

A Final Toast to Your Cotswolds Journey

As you tuck this book into your suitcase (next to that slightly muddy Ordnance Survey map and a dog-eared train ticket), remember: the Cotswolds isn't a destination you cross off. It's a place that seeps into your bones, a gentle nudge to live slower, look closer, and care deeper.

I'll leave you with a memory. Last autumn, I met a couple celebrating their 50th anniversary at **The Lygon Arms**. Over sherry, they confessed they'd honeymooned here in 1975. "Back then," the wife whispered, "we worried mass tourism would ruin it. But look—the hills are still golden, the pubs still warm. "Because people cared."

So here's my challenge to you: Care fiercely. Wander mindfully. And when you return home, bring the Cotswolds' rhythm with you—sip tea slower, greet strangers fuller, and maybe plant a lavender bush to remember the way the breeze smelled at Snowshill Manor.

The footpaths will always lead you back. And when you return, I'll be here—probably sipping a pint at The Porch House, ready to hear your stories.

Printed in Dunstable, United Kingdom